Inquiries should be addressed to:

D. Hall Books

1-313-808-3489

dhallbooks1@gmail.com

Cover Design:

The RJS Line.com
www.therjsline.com
313-673-2252

The Black Man's Journal:

Reflection, Growth, and Connection

By: Darrell Hall

Table of Contents

Chapter 1: A Black Man in A Blue City

Who Am I..5

Woodward Ave...6

Would I Still be a Nigga?..8

Chapter 2: Another Day Another Dollar and Another Day Helping Someone

Mom, you have to help too!..11

How DeShawn Brown become a Social Worker..13

He say, She say..16

7 Questions for Mr. Black and family..20

Chapter 3: I don't know what I did wrong, but I'm going to keep pushing on

Miss Twotone..23

An open letter to Lady T..25

The clean-up woman..26

One Tired Ass Black Man..27

Chapter 4: GOD is GOOD all the time and all the time GOD is GOOD

A letter to the Man upstairs...29

Moving Forward..31

Chapter 1:

A Black Man in A Blue City

Journal #1: Who AM I

I am the one that you closely watch and examine when entering your stores, schools, and neighborhoods. I am the descendant and brother of WEB Dubois, Paul Roberson, Michael Cartwright, Cornell West, Coleman Young, Jackie Robinson, Joe Louis, Robert Johnson, Tyler Perry, Steve Harvey, Joique Bell, Jamie Foxx, Dr. Frederick D. Haynes III, Bill Russell, George Washington Carver, Malcolm X, Dr. King, Denzel Washington, Langston Hughes, Muhammad Ali, Don Cheadle, Kareem, Booker T. Washington, and Hill Harper. Not only am I a prisoner of this often unjust system, but I am a high powered attorney and the commander and chief; keep pushing President Obama and thank you to Thurgood Marshall and Colin Powell.

I am the street pharmacies who often duck and dodge hot led and the boys in blue, but I am a graceful physician as well; an individual who can remove this hot led and diseases from my black body. Thank you to Dr. Carson, Dr. Drew, and Dr. Daniel Hale Williams for all your help and discoveries. This is the one I like the most. I am the one you love to hate, but not knowing why. Is it because of insecurities, your past encounters with my male siblings, or is it that I received too much attention? Yes, I created the stop sign and had much to do with the creation of the White House. I am the backbone of your country. I fly your planes and I remove your trash. It is I, who create and correct your streets, buildings, and cars when needed. And it is I who cause you to change so much. Like it or not, I am the one your kids admire; no matter if your kid is black, brown, yellow, white, or red. As you can see, I'm a bad MAN. I own every occupation under the sun and my skin tone and hair styles varies like no other people. I'm often misjudged, sometimes by my own people. What I am, A STRONG EDUCATED BLACK MAN.

Journal #2: WOODWARD AVE.

It's warm out, about 60-70 degree. A beautiful spring atmosphere is what I see on this particular Saturday. It's about two o'clock and my silver two-door Volvo is washed, my shades are clean, Dwele is in the CD player, and I still have the majority of my check left. So, let's reflect, visualize, take a trip to taste my favorite restaurant- Chipotle Mexican Grill, and do a little shopping for a bowtie or some burgundy pointy toe cowboy boots. I start off in my neighborhood, Woodward and I-75. Comerica Park, Ford Field, Hockey Town, and the Fox Theater are always wonderful places to visit. I continue north. Wayne State University is not that bad. They have an excellent social work and medical program. It's an urban and research university. Continue. The Detroit Institute of Arts, Detroit's Main Library, and the Detroit Historical Museum- can all be seen while driving down Woodward Avenue. Now I'm crossing over Grand Blvd, a police precinct is to the right and YouthVille is to the left. YouthVille is a cool place for little ones to hang out- mentoring, exercising, home-work assistance, games, sports, and Plymouth Educational High School- you name it they've got it. Down a little further, you will find Neighborhood Services Organization (I had to throw that in, I worked there for three years), Historical Little Rock Baptist Church, Northern High School/Pink Panther High school, and the Historic Boston Edison District(gigantic homes, I'm talking eight bedrooms). As we continue to drive north, we enter Highland Park. After leaving HP, we hit the back end of Palmer Woods, the construction site of the Winans' new kingdom- "Perfecting", and the State Fair Ground (soon to be known as Meijer's). As I cross over eight mile (still on Woodward Ave.), I'm introduced to the city of Ferndale. Some of the nice places in Ferndale and on Woodward Ave, include Toast (a small breakfast joint), the Rust Belt Market (nice art and vintage items), and Dino's Bar & Grill. Time to leave the city of Ferndale for the city of Royal Oak. As you enter Royal Oak you will see the Detroit Zoo on your left hand side. Down a couple blocks on the right, stands an outstanding, blue ribbon elementary/middle school- Shrine. Now that we have toured the cities of Royal Oak and Huntington Woods (I wouldn't mind living in either place- two beautiful cities), the expensive Birmingham is coming up next. Birmingham is the home to my favorite restaurant, Chipotle Mexican Grill, It's on Woodward and 14 mile Rd. I always get the chicken burrito- VERY GOOD. A few blocks down on the same side was Borders Bookstore; they carried a nice amount of black authors. I was able to eat sweets and review books, there's nothing like it. However, the Borders Company was removed. If one was to continue driving north on Woodward, he/she would cross Maple Rd. (15mile) and would be in walking distance of The Cranbrook School District, one of the most prestige schools in the state of the Michigan. A mile or two down from Cranbrook, is Pontiac, Michigan. Now it's time for me to turn back around, head south, and be on my way back to downtown Detroit- HOME.

Journal#3: Would I still be a Nigga

Would I still be a nigga

If I

If I decided to buy a Honda Civic or Toyota instead of a Chrysler or Cadillac with 24 inch chrome rims?

Would I still be a nigga

If I

If I decided to teach my son how to play soccer or an instrument, instead of basketball?

Would I still be a nigga

If I

If I decided to wear bowties and cowboy boots, instead of timberland boots and old English D baseball caps?

Would I still be a nigga

If I

If I spoke correct English and displayed appropriate manners, instead of calling everything muthafucka?

Would I still be a nigga

If I

If I watched the Cosby Show, instead of thinking such life is fake, unreal?

Would I still be a nigga

If I

If I didn't say the word, "nigga" like other niggas?

Would I still be a nigga?

Chapter 2:

Another Day Another Dollar and Another Day Helping Someone

Journal #1: Mom, you have to help too!

"Mr. Hall, I don't know what's wrong with my son. Sometimes he just sits there and stares at the wall. As you can see his grades are poor and he is failing most of his classes. And now he's smoking weed." This is what a mother cried out to me while sitting in my office; she is not the first or last parent with such a story. The mother and child are new to my caseload of 25 "at-risk" youth, families, or delinquents- whatever you wish to call them. The charges for this particular youth range from incorrigibility to school truancy. While the mother cried out for help, I could only think of the young man's relationship with other family members, his living conditions or environment, the biological father's where-a-bouts, and the mother's mental, emotional, and spiritual well-being.

As I continued to work with the family, which has not been that long, I noticed that the mother begin to justify the young man's lack of participation within the program. He was scheduled to participate in individual counseling, family sessions, and peer group meetings focusing on life skills, such as conflict resolution and decision making skills. The mother was consistently reminded that participation was mandatory, which was straight from the Judge. I would hear stories such as, "He don't feel like coming and I don't have any gas. This is too much for me, why should I have to meet, he's the one that's fucking up. Hell, I don't know where he at. He don't like the program. And y'all need to lock his lil black ass up!" WOW is right. I have always thought that kids were not bad; as my old professor once stated, "We are born a blank slate." Kids do what you allow them to do and they do what they see and if you don't provide positive support and supervision they're going to do what they want to do. Why should a kid attempt to do better in school if he or she is rewarded for earning a 1.5gpa, with gym shoes, jeans, or a new cell phone? As a case worker I see situations like this all the time .For some parents, it's the schools fault. Yes, some school districts are not preforming well, but mom and dad you have to do your part as well .Assist with homework if you can (don't believe your child doesn't have homework) and communicate with your child's teacher. Excuse my tone, but I would have pissed all the way home if I received a, "D" or "F" on my report card. Everyone must be held accountable for the lack of progress. Mothers please email your child's teachers, attend parent-teacher conferences, and reward your babies for receiving As and Bs. And mothers make your home a place of peace and love. In regards to the kids, what you put in, is what you receive. Reader, you have to help too!

Journal #2: How DeShawn Brown became a Social Worker

You don't have to be rich or white to want to help people. After watching most of these movies out here, one would think that most of the people providing assistance where white and the only people causing trouble were every other race. You don't have to be the product of a two-parent household or possess a doctoral degree to want to change lives, save lives, or hope for change. A little secret, agents for change come in all different shapes, sizes, ages, and colors. If you don't believe me attend a social work class at Wayne State University. You can be an ex-convict, dancer, or garbage man and still wish to change lives and hope for the best. In the case of DeShawn, his mother is white and his father is black. Both parents were educated and hoped that DeShawn would pursue a career in the business field or something that was white-collar, with a black or blue tie, and sit behind a desk for seven point five hours a day. Well, the parents had no idea that raising DeShawn in such a city would cause him to become curious of the behaviors and attitudes of others.

Throughout grade school, DeShawn received passing grades, participated in school activities, and appeared to be excited about attending college. In regards to his friends, well they just came and left; one can say it was a seasonal thing. He would always express that Michigan State University was the place to be and they had an excellent Criminal Justice program. Leaving whatever peers behind to improve self was just something that had to happen. His plans were to leave the so-called "hood", which was as colorful as a bag of M &Ms, but harder than jaw-breakers, attend Michigan State to study Criminal Justice and play baseball. Well after leaving the so called "hood", DeShawn did just that, attended Michigan State

University and blew the Criminal Justice department out the water. He received the opportunity to visit several correctional facilities, court houses, and participate in ride-a-longs with the local police department. The CIA and ATF appeared to be in arms reach.

Every summer returning home from school, he noticed the lack of progress and happiness in the neighborhood. In fact more and more homes appeared to be vacant and the Chrsyler families were exchanged for low income families. The once active block club had lost its name. The late summer nights on the porch would bring WOWS and OHHHS to DeShawn's curiosity of human behavior and the black family. Although the conversations on the porch with his mother consisted of, "Have you thought about an office job at Chrysler? What about working at the bank? Or law firm?"DeShawn continued to be interested in the reasons behind his peer's behaviors and the reasons why the community appeared to be so negative and dense. With these questions of what, when, why, where, and how, as they relate to his declining neighborhood, the ideas of working as a federal law enforcement officer was placed on the back burner .His new career path would focus on human services and social services. The idea of kicking down doors and yelling, "get on the floor" and "where are the drugs?" was no longer interesting. Mentoring, educating, providing resources, and spreading the word were now his primary focus.

Currently, DeShawn is a psychology professor at a local community college and clinical therapist at a local mental health agency. In addition, he has created mentoring services in his old neighborhood entitled, "Flying High". According to Deshawn, it's not about where you come from; it's about where you're going.

Journal #3: He say, She say

"There's a direct correlation between parental involvement and school success, so I decided to write this proposal. We've got to start somewhere. It's going to be a hard sell- although I don't think a 15 minute visit, a phone call or an email once a year to your child's teacher is too much to ask."

-Kym Worthy (Detroit Prosecutor)

Essence Magazine

March 2011

"Its better to be single wanting to be married than it is to be married wanting to be single"

-Tony Evans

Being Single and Satisfied

2002

"I know what a woman feels when she says she feels like a piece of meat, first hand and when I was younger, I probably would have thought that that was what I wanted. You get older, then you start realizing ugh."

Anthony Hamilton

Sister to Sister

June 2004

"I wake up with myself every morning, so the only opinion that really matter is mine."

-Gabourey Sidibe (Precious)

Ebony

March 2010

"If momma don't have self-respect, interigerty or dignity for herself, then how is she going to teach them to her daughter. When momma chooses the wrong men to sleep with and have their babies, how can she teach her daughter to choose a good man."

-Theresa McMiller (Indianapolis, IN)

Ebony Magazine

May 2007

"We are constructed to have very low expectations of ourselves- our abilities and capacities for deep intellectual, spiritual, and emotional growth. Thus our citizenship claim can be easily revoked at the slightest infraction – or jaywalking or not wearing tie- without so much as a doubt."

-Rohan Preston

Not Guilty- Twelve Black Men Speak out on Law, Justice, and Life

2001

"We can't change our past, but we can start fresh with good family names, good values and good habits we're proud to pass from generation to generation. Let's change what's bad and keep the good stuff"

- Tom Joyner (Ebony Magzine July 2011)

"A younger person may be swayed by the externals, by the front that the other person puts up. But godly father who is walking with the Lord can help his daughter see the real deal in a potential husband, and he can demand some serious commitments from the man who desires to marry his daughter"

-Tony Evans

Being Single and Satisfied 2002

"Its not a matter of temptation. All men are tempted. It's a matter of self-control and self-discipline"

-T.D. Jakes

So You Call Yourself A Man?

1997

"I know someone who has a nine-year old son and a fourteen year old girl whom she allows to see her heavy casual-dating lifestyle. She allows a few of her male acquaintances to come over to her house for "visits". She is teaching her son that this is what men do-run up in and out of a woman's house without commitment. She's training her daughter how to run drive-thru relationships and that its okay to give up a little to get a little. Kids do not do what you say, they do what you do."

-Ty Adams

Single, Saved, and Having Sex

2003

Journal #4   7 Questions for Mr. Black and Family

Mr. Black, I have seven questions for you and your family.

Question 1: Mr. Black, can we stop fighting each other over grandma's money and house? I think the most important things for grandma are health, stability, support, and safety.

Question2: Mr. Black, can we slowly learn to trust each other? You trust the Whitestones' with your money, the Lees' for your beauty needs, and the Abdul family for everything else. Why not trust me, Mr. Johnson.

Question 3: Ok Mr. Black, I know you go to church on Sundays and sometimes on Wednesday, but can you live accordingly to what is being taught at Bible study and Sunday school? For example Mr. Black, I have observed your family members blasting the Clark sisters, Tamela Mann, and Kirk Franklin, but they don't speak to their co-workers; hell they barely speak to their family members.

Questions 4: Mr. Black, can we embrace the idea of, "African and African American History?" I was once told, "In order to understand the present, you must know the past."

Question 5: Mr. Black, I know it's going to be hard, but can we begin to save money? I know it's hard, I have tried on several occasions.

Question 6: Mr. Black, can we begin to decrease our patients for negativity? For example Mr. Black we can stay in a negative relationship for years, but find every reason in the world to stay out of a positive relationship or return to school.

Question 7: Mr. Black, what can we do to improve the black family?

Chapter 3:

I don't know what I did wrong, but I'm going to keep pushing on

Journal #1: Miss Twotone

A couple of years ago I attended a New Year's Eve service in the city of HardKnock. What a site. What an experience. The church was the size of a classroom. Out of the 60 members or visitors, 45 of them were 30yrs of age or younger. Out of the 45, 40 had a child or children that appeared to be 10 years of age or younger. To continue, out of the 40 that had a child, half of them appeared to be pregnant. As I sat in the last row, I noticed a number of young single mothers. What I did not notice was a significant male on her side. And these young ladies appeared to be full of the spirit. They moved to the music, sweated their hair loose, and praised HIM freely. Although it was a small church and had majority young saints, IT WAS ROCKING. I can say for the most part, I really enjoyed myself. Going to church and seeing young mothers with their babies and no significant other by her side is not a new view in some places. After the rocking, the praising, the dancing, and the music stopped that was after 3 hours, it was time for the word; the part I like. At this point the scenery changed. Minutes into the word, babies begin to be passed around, heads were constantly moving right to left and left to right, every IPhone and Galaxy was up and running, and tablets were a cover up for the downloaded bibles. Yeah, you can see a lot sitting in the second from last row. But I must say the pastor was good. He spoke about standards, decision making, and goal setting; I love it. It appeared that when he spoke of these matters, the joy and praising came to a halt. I don't know why and I didn't want to offend anyone by asking why.

Several months after my New Year's Eve excitement and experience, I encountered a young lady who also appeared to be full of the spirit. We met at a training, which was held at a non-profit organization in Detroit. She was speaking to one of my co-workers about her busy week, returning to school, and attending church. I asked what church did she attend and what was she going to school for? She was trying to return to the school that I recently departed from- Wayne State University. We continue to chat and exchanged phone numbers. After several conversations on the telephone, the topic of sex came up. WOW. I was asked, "Do you believe in sex before marriage?" No matter what I said, I should have said, "NO"; maybe we would still be communicating to this day. I think not. I think I will continue to be truthful with myself and others. Yes, young lady I have had sex before and I cannot take it back. SORRY. I am not a 304.In fact, I treat some sisters better than "some" treat themselves. What I am is human and respectful.

My encounters with Miss Twotone began before that New Year 's Eve event or training session. It actually started two years after leaving the University of Michigan. At that time, she stopped my quest for her heart after saying, "I can't be with you, because you don't speak in tongue- so I cannot pray with you." This came after informing her that I was trying to learn more about the Bible and attend church more. Miss Twotone continued when her family rejected me for not attending their church on a regular basis; although I was attending my own church. According to her family, "If I truly cared for her I would attend their church and participate on a regular basis." It appears that no matter how supportive and positive I am, Miss Twotone will find a way to leave. I'm not attending their churches on a regular, but she's not pleased with the brothers that are attending their church 3x a week either.

Journal #2: An open letter to Lady T (My Ex)

Dear Lady T,

This letter is based on our relationship, no sexship- that's the only thing we didn't have a problem with. Sweetheart, either you have no substance or lost in the subject of relationshipology- believing that to keep a man, a woman must cook and provide sexual favors. WOW. Well babe you forgot about the support, communication, and spiritual side. I never understood, how can you perform oral sex on a person and never ask, "How was your day?" or "How you feeling?" Listen Lady T, I care about you probably more than you care about yourself. So, saying that I want to help you in some type of form to be in a healthy, equal, and productive relationship.

- Before anything else, be real with self and love self (You can't change or save the world, but you can save yourself from destruction).
- Understand the definition of love (Actions speaks louder than words. Some say you must see love growing up in order to give it, or receive it).
- Control your anger and aggression (Find the source).
- Ask your mate questions about his past, present, and future.

Remember there are people who care, who support you, and who love you. Remember, you're priceless. Remember, you're a queen.

Journal #3: The clean-up woman

I thank you, I thank you for your services. I thank you for the cleaning of other's trash and their dust from confrontations. I thank you for the males and conversations after a 12 round tussling-control match. Your talks, magical bandages, and stability, help heal my scares and wounds that were obtained during the fight, for that I thank you. Your style of cleaning and caring for a family is remarkable. You sat back, observed your mother, and watched the mistakes made by peers. When it was your time to perform; you did a hell of a job. You did just that- Perform. It is obvious that you do not need 409, AJAX, or Bleach, your substance, purity, and soul is more than enough. Your substance, purity, and soul were able to remove the stains and pains that once covered my body and home. Your substance provided me with the energy and excitement to fight another 12rounds. Sometime, we don't give you praise, and often look down to those who clean other people sh*t, like custodians or garbage collectors. If you have not heard it before, you are about to hear it now- THANK YOU AND I appreciate IT.I don't know how you do it or why you do it, but I guess one can say that you are a special one sent from the Man upstairs; GOD. Your drive to become a better mother, a better student, and a better woman only provides me with more reasons to love you.

THANK YOU MISS CLEAN UP WOMAN

Journal #4: One Tired ass Black Man

I have tried writing you a three page letter expressing my care and feelings for you and your family. You completely ignored the letter-literally.

I thought sending you flowers and balloons would help; nope no luck.

I have tried to communicate and not have sex on the first night. That only pushed you away.

I did not mind helping you with your little one or little ones, but I guess you did not believe me because you have heard it all before.

I have tried to support your educational and career goals, but I think that was being too nosey.

I have never asked you for money or oral sex and you never had to compete with my baby momma or wife; I don't have those.

It's ok. I will still love you. I will still support you. And I will still show you how special you are.

But, I am one tired ass black man.

Chapter 4: GOD is GOOD all the time and all the time GOD is GOOD

Journal #1: A letter to the Man upstairs

To the Man upstairs:

When I need someone to talk to, when I can't get negative thoughts out of my head, or when I need to be uplifted, I can always read literature or music on your behalf. I never go wrong when I pick up a book or listen to a song and someone is expressing how good you have been to them or you are the source for growth, light, and happiness. Wow. Now I cannot lie, I get off track at times- trying to solve my own problems, trying to fight my own battles, and trying to find my own mate; instead of focusing on the one and only that can led me to my queen- You. With my face down and my knees bent, I have thanked you, asked for strength, asked for patience, asked for you to show me the way, and asked to be a better man, and I asked for a wife. I'm in the progress of learning and growing- mentally, physically, emotionally, and spiritually. Yes, it's hard but I'm making progress, with your help. As you know, I have been in a lot of negative relationships, which ended quickly. On the outside I shake my head or may shed a tear or two, but deep down, I thank you for the interruption- it was needed for my development, growth, and understanding of the world and the people in it. Thank you! As I am sitting here writing, I have reflected on how you have taught me to be humble in situations, give first, forgive those who have betrayed me, and to love as you love the church. No matter my experiences, rejections, disappointments, or betrayals, I will continue to try to live by your word. I will continue to be a supporter and give with an open heart. I will continue to be humble and continue to love. I will always treat people with the utmost respect, even if they don't respect and love themselves. I will continue to grow and seek your power to be the best man of God that I can be. I have to seek you and your power and your light- so that I can be the best father and husband I hope to be. I will not just lay on my face, bow down before you, or lift my arms to you until my prayers are answer. But I WILL ALWAYS SEEK YOU and I WILL Always communicate with you and Thank You.

Sincerely,

Darrell Jermaine Hall.

Journal #2 Moving Forward

I don't know where I will be in the next 12months. I am unsure of marriage and unsure if I will be able to call Detroit home. But what I do know is that I have a lot to be thankful for. We all have tough times and good and bad people in our lives, but I would like to focus on the good; the people who provided me with the opportunity to shine, grow, and most of all- be myself. I also know that I will continue to do three things: 1.) Pray (Strength and to be led to my wife) 2.) Help my people (I can't see myself doing anything else) 3.) Learn. These three things of praying, helping, and learning will never stop no matter where this journey takes me- to Nashville, Tennessee, Charlotte, North Carolina, Bloomfield Hills, or to Africa- Back home.

Notes

www.ingramcontent.com/pod-product-compliance
Ingram Content Group UK Ltd.
Pitfield, Milton Keynes, MK11 3LW, UK
UKHW020227250726
13967UKWH00001B/236

9 781304 145109